)

THE AMERICAN
PRAIRIE CHICKEN

OTHER BOOKS BY MARY ADRIAN

Hastings House

THE KITE MYSTERY

THE INDIAN HORSE MYSTERY

THE MYSTERY OF THE DINOSAUR BONES

THE SKIN DIVING MYSTERY

THE MYSTERY OF THE NIGHT EXPLORERS

THE RARE STAMP MYSTERY

THE FOX HOLLOW MYSTERY

THE URANIUM MYSTERY

THE PRESERVE OUR WILDLIFE SERIES

THE AMERICAN EAGLE

THE AMERICAN MUSTANG

THE NORTH AMERICAN WOLF

THE NORTH AMERICAN BIGHORN SHEEP

THE AMERICAN ALLIGATOR

THE BALANCE OF NATURE SERIES

A DAY AND A NIGHT IN A FOREST

Holiday House

GARDEN SPIDER

HONEYBEE

FIDDLER CRAB

GRAY SQUIRREL

Houghton Mifflin Company

THE FIREHOUSE MYSTERY

THE TUGBOAT MYSTERY

PRESERVE OUR WILDLIFE SERIES

THE
AMERICAN PRAIRIE CHICKEN

BY
MARY ADRIAN

Illustrated by
Genevieve Vaughan-Jackson

HASTINGS HOUSE • PUBLISHERS

NEW YORK

I wish to express my sincere thanks to Valgene W. Lehmann for reading and criticizing the manuscript of this book. Mr. Lehmann is a recognized authority on prairie chickens in the United States. He is Wildlife Manager of the King Ranch in Texas and currently is spending full time planning restoration projects for prairie chickens.

MARY ADRIAN

Published simultaneously in Canada by Saunders, of Toronto, Ltd., Don Mills, Ontario.

Library of Congress Catalog Card Number: 68-21353
Printed in the United States of America

FOREWORD

The prairie chicken lives on the central and western plains of the United States. There are two species: the greater prairie chicken and the lesser prairie chicken. The Attwater prairie chicken is a subspecies (a race or variety) of the greater prairie chicken, and they are all members of the grouse family.

The Latin name for the greater prairie chicken is *Tympanuchus cupido americanus.* It is a large henlike bird, barred in light and dark brown. The male has orange air sacs on the side of the neck.

The lesser prairie chicken, *Tympanuchus pallidicinctus,* is smaller and lighter in color, with dull red air sacs.

The Attwater prairie chicken, *Tympanuchus cupido attwateri,* looks like the greater prairie chicken except that it is slightly smaller and darker in color. Its eggs, nesting habits, courtship dancing and booming calls are similar to those of the other species.

The life cycle of the Attwater prairie chicken is the one described in this book because this bird is almost extinct. It was named by Major Charles E. Bendire in 1894 in honor of his friend, Professor H. W. Attwater.

At one time the Attwater prairie chicken could range over six million acres of prairie along the Gulf Coast from Southern Texas northeastward to Louisiana. It has been estimated that once there were over one million of these birds. Today there is none in Louisiana, and only about one thousand remain in Texas.

Their near-extermination began late in the nineteenth century when cattlemen hunted the Attwater prairie chicken not only for meat, but for sport. Large numbers of them were killed within a few hours in "shoots" and piles of them were left to decay or to be eaten by vultures.

However, the main reason for the Attwater prairie chicken's decline in population is that its native prairies have been turned into crop lands. It cannot adapt itself to new environments as some birds do. It depends upon the cover of the tall prairie grass for its needs, but since its feeding areas and nesting grounds have excellent soil for grazing and for growing rice and cotton, man has taken it over for himself at the expense of this now rare bird.

All prairie chickens are threatened with a similar fate.

Some effort is now being made to save the Attwater prairie chicken. Texas Wildlife, an affiliate of World Wildlife Fund, has launched a campaign to buy land and set aside a sanctuary where a breeding stock of prairie chickens still exists.

Swan Lake National Wildlife Refuge in Missouri, Valentine National Wildlife Refuge in Nebraska, and Upper Souris National Wildlife Refuge in North Dakota offer protection to the greater prairie chicken. But other areas of natural grasslands should be set aside for both species of the prairie chickens.

A number of our American birds have vanished. Among them are the great auk, the passenger pigeon, and the heath hen. It is sad to know that you and I will never see these birds. Let us hope that we will always have the prairie chicken with us. It deserves protection if only as the symbol of our prairies.

Salem, Oregon   Mary Adrian

1

THE HUNTER

Years ago on a summer afternoon a flock of Attwater prairie chickens were feeding among the tall grass along the Gulf Coast of Texas. Cocks, hens, and their young pecked at insects and seeds, moving slowly through the open land where the hot sun beat down upon them. Their feathers, barred with dark and light brown, blended with their surroundings, the high grass. This was the only protection the prairie chickens had from their enemies.

They were aware of this for they often stopped eating and stretched their necks to look about anxiously. Even the youngsters were on the alert for danger.

Soon the shadow of a passing cloud made the

flock uneasy. They stared at the sky and then squatted in the high grass as a turkey vulture flew overhead. He wanted to find the meat of dead animals and so flew onward. The flock relaxed and again started eating the ripe grass seeds that had fallen to the ground.

Soon the prairie chickens quietly moved on, lifting one foot at a time, until they heard a noise close-by. Was it a wolf or a coyote? They were the most dreaded enemies.

Instantly the prairie chickens stood so still they looked like statues. Not a muscle moved until an armadillo shuffled into view. He was covered with an armor of small bony plates. He hunted mostly at night for grasshoppers and bugs.

Right now his keen scent had led him to an ant hill. Grunting, he flicked out his sticky tongue and licked up some of the scrambling insects.

The flock watched him for a while and then walked through more high grass, pushing the tall blades aside and stopping often to feed.

Finally, where the grass was thin and short, they came upon another animal. It was a striped ground squirrel. He was standing bolt upright by the doorway to his burrow, looking around for danger.

Suddenly he whistled shrilly and dove into his hole. He had just spotted two Indians on horseback in the distance. Armed with bows and arrows, they were chasing a herd of deer.

The prairie chickens ran for the tall grass. Some nearly knocked each other down in their haste, but in a few moments not a bird could be seen. Even the youngsters looked like lumps of earth as they crouched. Terrified, they listened to the sound of horses' hoofs beating the ground.

In leaps and bounds with their white tails flashing behind them, the deer headed for some brush, but the Indians killed two of them before they reached it. The red men needed the hides of the animals for clothing and the meat for food.

Time went by. The prairie chickens still kept quiet. Grasshoppers jumped around them. They would make good eating, but the flock did not budge. They waited until the Indians were far away, and there was silence. Then the prairie chickens popped up, one after another and looked around. They could see the striped ground squirrel standing upright next to his burrow. He had come out of hiding and would warn them if there was more danger.

The flock did not hear his sharp whistle, so they moved into the shadows made by the late afternoon sun. They walked quietly through the tall grass until they came to a small pond where a great blue heron was feeding. She was a large bird with stilt-like legs.

After making sure that all was safe, the prairie chickens lined up in a row on the shore. They dipped up water in their bills, threw back their heads, and swallowed. Then they bowed again to take another drink.

A few hens watched their young play among the wild flowers. Because the wind was blowing away from them, they were not aware that an Indian boy was creeping toward them through the high grass. He knew the game trails leading to water, and now he saw his chance to shoot his first bird. Crouching low, the boy moved a few steps more.

Just then the watchful heron saw the young Indian. With loud squawks she took to the air. Her hoarse cries rang out loud and clear, but her warning came too late. The boy had pulled back the string on his bow and sent an arrow through the air. It struck a prairie hen in the side and killed her instantly.

With a whirr of wings the flock scattered. Crazed with fear, they flew in different directions and hid in the tall grass.

The Indian boy was not interested in hunting more prairie chickens. He had shot his first bird, and he knew his parents would be proud of him.

As he hurried back to his village camp with his kill, the flock moved cautiously through the sea of golden grass. They stopped and listened to the cry of a wolf out hunting, but since his call sounded far away, the prairie chickens quietly moved on. Through more open land they went —cocks, hens, and their young until they came to a sheltered place under some bushes where they roosted for the night.

2

THE COURTING GROUNDS

Seasons came and went on the coastal prairie of Texas, but not many Attwater prairie chickens roamed on the open land any more. That was because the white men had hunted these choice game birds both for food and for sport and had killed many thousands of them. Now, only the descendents of the few who had escaped were living there.

One March morning twelve cocks awakened before sunrise at their roosting places on the ground in the high grass. They flew to their courting stations on a nearby area of "hard pan" soil where the grass was very short. It was about two acres in size.

Each male cackled as he settled on his own section. This was a few square yards of the courting grounds.

Finally the roosters were ready to dance and give the mating call. This is known as *booming*. By letting the air out of the orange sacs on each side of their necks, the males make hollow booming sounds.

Just as one cock started to lead the dance, another rooster moved in on his courting station. Feathers raised and eyes snapping, the owner rushed toward the trespasser. Beak to beak they stood, ready to fight like two barnyard roosters.

They separated, cackled loudly, and seesawed back and forth. They leaped into the air and struck each other with their wings and feet.

When they landed on the ground, the owner of the station grabbed one of the stranger's feathers in his bill and pulled it out.

The cock squawked. He had had enough. He turned and ran away.

The owner looked around. No other rooster seemed about to come on his territory, so he smoothed down his ruffled plumage.

At dawn the next day the twelve roosters met again on their courting grounds. Since late February they had boomed there each day in the early morning and before sunset. The hens had paid no attention to their booming calls, but now that the March days were warm, they were showing interest.

One hen started walking toward the courtship grounds. Prairie Chicken was a beautiful one-year-old bird. The chestnut colored feathers on her neck glistened in the early morning light.

Her slender neck was not adorned with bright orange air sacs like the males, and she was somewhat smaller.

Prairie Chicken continued walking slowly until she came within view of the roosters.

One cock was about to begin the dance. With head low, tail spread, and wings drooping he ran a few steps forward. He paused and began stamping on the ground. Jerking violently, the rooster made a booming noise as his orange air sacks deflated like pricked balloons. Then the cock patted the ground with his feet and puffed out his air sacs again. As he released the air, "Boom! Boom! Boom!" rang out loud and clear.

The other roosters joined in, dancing and giving their mating calls. These could be heard a mile or more away. Faster and faster the birds stamped. Louder and louder their booms sounded as the cocks noticed Prairie Chicken and gave her their welcome. They forgot about defending the boundaries of their courting stations. Instead, they rushed up and strutted around her. They jumped up and down and flapped their wings.

Prairie Chicken did not seem impressed. Circling around the males, she left the area and continued on her way.

Soon several other hens came to the courting grounds. They stayed to be mated.

At dawn the next morning Prairie Chicken visited the courting grounds. This time she strolled past several males who were stamping and booming to get her attention.

3

TWELVE EGGS

Prairie Chicken wandered through the high grass, hunting for a suitable place for her nest. Many birds have the help of their mates, but Prairie Chicken, like others of her kind, had to build her nest and raise her young alone.

In a little while she found a small hollow in the ground, but it was not big enough for her to sit in. So she walked on, pushing more grass blades aside and stopping every few moments to see if her movements had attracted the attention of an enemy.

Soon Prairie Chicken decided to make her own hollow in the earth near a grassy knoll. She pecked and scratched at the soft soil until she had formed a small bowl. She sat down in the cavity. Satisfied that it was the right shape and size for her plump body, she got up and lined the nest with dead grass and weeds. After that Prairie Chicken laid her first olive-gray egg, about an inch and a half long.

The next morning Prairie Chicken laid another egg. She did not lay any the next day, but by the end of three weeks twelve eggs filled the nest.

Prairie Chicken was ready now to sit on the eggs. She fluffed out the feathers on her breast and sides to cover them. She squirmed to make herself comfortable. Then, looking like a small pillow, she held very still so that her scent would not come through her plumage and tell an enemy where her nest was hidden in the high grass.

All was quiet around her until a meadowlark sang near her nest. After he had finished his song, Prairie Chicken saw a cricket crawling along the ground. The insect was only a morsel of food to her, but it would taste very good at the

moment. However, she did not want to leave her eggs in the noon-day sun. The scorching heat would harm the embryos forming inside the shells.

Suddenly a grasshopper landed on a short weed in front of Prairie Chicken. The temptation was too great. She reached far out of the nest, grabbed the insect, and ate it. After that she settled back on her eggs and was about to doze when she heard a crow caw. Crows eat birds' eggs, but Prairie Chicken felt she had nothing to fear as long as she stayed on the nest.

There was another sound, though, that disturbed her—the hum of a distant tractor. A farmer was plowing the earth to plant crops. Far into the afternoon Prairie Chicken heard the noise of his machine.

When it was quiet again on the prairie, she felt at ease. Not for long, however. Suddenly she saw something move in the tall grass—something with yellowish-brown fur.

It was a coyote, who ate not only eggs but game birds as well.

Prairie Chicken froze with fright. Not a feather moved. Not an eyelid blinked.

The coyote paused and looked about him. He took a few steps in Prairie Chicken's direction, but he did not see her because her feathers blended with the color of the dead weeds and dry grass around her.

The coyote raised his head and sniffed the air. No scent came back to him. Slowly he walked on. He went past Prairie Chicken sitting on her eggs without knowing she was there.

Prairie Chicken did not budge until she felt the coyote was a safe distance away.

Soon an orange glow settled over the prairie. The sun was sinking in the west. Prairie Chicken looked carefully about her to make sure no spying enemy was near. Then quietly she slipped off her nest to have her first good meal since morning.

4

THE FIRST HUNT

For about three weeks Prairie Chicken sat on her eggs, turning them now and then with her bill so that they would be evenly warmed. But only in early morning and before dusk did she leave the nest for food.

Now, on the twenty-second day she became greatly excited. She heard tiny peepings within the eggshells. Prairie Chicken reached under her breast feathers and turned over the eggs not once but many times that day.

The next morning twelve chicks peeped and pushed inside the eggshells. They wanted to get out of their prison. Finally, one chick tapped very hard with a tiny white egg tooth at the end of his bill. He would lose this tooth the next day,

but right now it was a handy tool. With it he cut a crack in the big end of the shell. Then he tapped and pushed some more. The crack grew wider and wider, and out tumbled the chick. He was followed by eleven other chicks, all crowded together in the nest like peas in a pod.

Their down was wet, but Prairie Chicken cuddled her babies under her wings in the nest until they were dry.

First one chick and then two others poked their tiny heads through her plumage and peered at the outside world.

Before long one youngster climbed up on his mother's back. Even though it was slippery, he stayed on top, looking like a ball of yellow fluff mottled in brown. With a triumphant peep, he stood gazing around until one of his brothers came and pushed him off. Then the brother, too, slid off the slippery perch, but both chicks managed to keep on their feet.

By this time Prairie Chicken decided that her brood was ready to leave the nest forever. She got up, stretched one leg, and then the other. She

shook her tail feathers and, after ruffling the rest of her plumage, gave a clucking call.

The ten other chicks scrambled out of the nest. They ran among the flowers and grasses. Some bumped into each other and fell down, but they all stayed close to their mother, who made low soft noises to keep them from straying away.

After a while the chicks began to peep. It was not because they were hungry. The egg yolk left in their bodies satisfied them. They were just tired from their first outing, so they crept under their mother's feathers and went to sleep on the ground.

The next morning, when Prairie Chicken felt it was warm enough, she took her chicks on their first hunting trip, along a trail made by cattle in the high grass. The youngsters examined weed stalks and flowers and found bugs, which they snatched up in their tiny bills. They caught small grasshoppers but tore them apart and swallowed each piece whole because they had not teeth to chew the meat.

In a short while one youngster wandered off. It was not long before she saw a raccoon, a plump, bushy-haired animal, come out of the brush. He was a night prowler, but occasionally he hunted in the daytime, and sometimes he ate poultry and young birds.

The raccoon looked so enormous to the tiny chick that she peeped in alarm.

Her mother came running. Before she could

reach her baby, a Cooper's hawk flying overhead had spotted the chick. There are several different kinds of hawks that do a lot of good by eating rats and mice, but Cooper's hawk also raids the farmers' barnyards and feeds on prairie chickens.

Like a thunderbolt from the sky, Cooper's hawk dropped down and grabbed the youngster in his talons.

As he flew away with his prey, Prairie Chicken warned her other chicks of danger. Little as they were, they froze in their tracks. Their mother also did the same, because she knew that the hawk or the raccoon could easily kill a full-grown prairie chicken.

Minutes passed. The raccoon growled and grumbled to himself. At last he went back into the brush.

As soon as Prairie Chicken felt it was safe to move about, she called to her eleven chicks. They sprang back to life at once. They ran here and there in the sunshine with the wind blowing the grasses.

5

DRAGGING
A WING

The chicks were several days old now. They looked like pincushions with their pinfeathers showing through their down. The youngsters scurried here and there, hunting bugs while their mother watched for enemies.

Soon black clouds appeared in the north. At first they were small, but as they grew larger, rain fell from the heavens. It drenched the youngsters before they could reach their mother. Peeping shrilly, they scrambled under her wings in the shelter of a tumbleweed and huddled there while the storm raged.

In the afternoon the rain turned into a drizzle and the temperature began dropping. By the next morning it was very cold.

Prairie Chicken tried her best to keep her chicks warm, but it was hard to wrap her feathers around all of them. They were bigger now than when they were born.

Through that day and night she struggled to take care of her brood. When morning brought sunlight, Prairie Chicken got up and clucked softly to her babies. Only eight chicks answered her. During the cold rainy spell, without any food, three of them had died.

The following week the remaining youngsters grew fast. They flapped their tiny new wings as they ran along the ground. Suddenly they found that their wings were holding them up in the air. The chicks flew a few feet and landed on the ground, peeping proudly.

It was not long, though, before one youngster peeped more loudly. He was lost. All he could see around him was brush.

Prairie Chicken heard his frantic call. She hurried to his side and led him back to the others. Then, while still on the lookout for danger, she

watched a pair of mourning doves who had nested on a small knoll close-by. They were busy feeding their brood.

Presently a scissortail flycatcher landed on a dead branch of an oak tree near the knoll. In a few moments he left his perch and swooped down to seize a grasshopper near Prairie Chicken. He rose in the air and, opening and closing his tail feathers like a pair of scissors, flew to a fence post a short distance away.

After that a gray cat prowled nearby, looking for food. The high grass kept Prairie Chicken from seeing the cat, who soon spotted the chicks scampering about. He lay perfectly still, waiting for a youngster to come his way.

Before long one chick headed for a flower near the place where the cat was hiding. The little prairie chicken looked at the underside of the flower and found a bug to eat. She took one step then another. Now she was only a few feet away from the cat. Too late she saw the gleaming eyes of her enemy.

The cat pounced on the youngster like the spring of a trap.

The chick cried out in terror and beat one tiny wing trying to get away.

A second later Prairie Chicken flew into the cat's face. He was so startled that he dropped the chick. She ran to hide in the tall weeds.

The other youngsters stayed very still, squatting in the high grass.

Prairie Chicken was not finished with the cat. With shrill squawks, she dragged one of her wings as though she were wounded. It was a trick that she played with enemies.

The gray cat was fooled. He began following Prairie Chicken.

She let him come almost within reach of her. Then she flew off with a whirr of wings and landed a few yards away.

The cat moved after Prairie Chicken. She allowed him to get close before she took off again. Prairie Chicken kept doing this until she had led the animal a safe distance from her youngsters.

After that she left a puzzled gray cat and circled back to her brood who were still hiding. She waited, watched, and finally called to them that all danger was past.

Her chicks scurried toward her and then looked in alarm at a cottontail rabbit who had jumped out of a thicket close-by.

Prairie Chicken clucked softly to tell her youngsters not to fear him.

They watched the rabbit bounce along. When he stopped to nibble on some clover, the chicks gathered around him. They seemed glad that they had found a neighbor who was not an enemy.

6

THE PRAIRIE FIRES

It was midsummer. The young prairie chickens were fully feathered, and were beginning to look like grown-up birds. They ate fewer bugs now. Seeds of grasses and weeds were more to their liking.

Prairie Chicken still tried to protect her brood from enemies, but in spite of her careful watching, a wild dog killed three of them. Only five youngsters were left of Prairie Chicken's twelve.

One morning she decided to take a dust bath. She scratched at the soft soil and worked it into her feathers to clean them.

Her chicks watched her, and then they rolled on their sides and sifted the loose dust into *their* plumage. It made them feel good.

Around them the parched grass waved in the hot winds. Rain had not fallen in many weeks, and the prairie was as dry as tissue paper.

Soon a burrowing owl came out of his hole in the ground and looked at the five young prairie chickens. They stared back at him and then looked beyond at a white-tailed deer and her fawn bounding through the high grass.

After that a wild turkey came into view. He too stopped to take a dust bath. As he strutted off, the quiet of the prairie was broken by the droning noise of a farmer's combine harvester. The machine was moving over a nearby field, cutting and threshing the ripened grain.

Suddenly it backfired and a spark, carried by the wind, dropped into some dry grass several yards away. A flame shot up in the air. In a few moments tongues of red were leaping here and there through a curtain of smoke.

Prairie Chicken knew there was only one thing to do—fly away from the fire, which was coming in her direction.

The wild turkey already had taken to the air. He was a strong flyer and could sail a mile with only a few wing beats. Prairie Chicken could fly only a short distance at a time. She gathered her youngsters around her and they made short flights together.

They flew by the cottontail rabbit who was running in terror to escape the fire. He no longer feared the coyote, who was his enemy but who was also hurrying to get away from the flames. There were even mice running alongside the gray cat.

Overhead the scissortail flycatcher darted past Prairie Chicken and her brood, who had stopped

to rest. They had caught up with some other prairie chickens—cocks, hens, and young.

Just as the flock was about to fly on, they saw flames ahead. Another fire had started because a person had carelessly thrown a lighted cigarette into a bed of dry grass.

Prairie Chicken did not know which way to turn. Could she and her youngsters escape this

second fire? She led her brood to the left only
to find a dense wall of smoke. Desperate, they
turned and flew right, toward a slope.

By this time men were fighting the two fires.
Some were driving bulldozers to make a fire-
break and clear the land so that there would be

nothing to burn. Others were using sacks to beat out the flames.

Fortunately, the hot winds soon died down, and after several hours the fires were out.

Prairie Chicken and her brood were alive. They looked out on a blackened land where toads, lizards, and snakes were badly singed. Some animals whose burrows were not deep had suffocated and died.

At nightfall Prairie Chicken and her five youngsters flew to a damp low place that had escaped the fire. They roosted on the ground among the grasses and sedges with some other prairie chickens.

The next morning the flock made short flights through the fire-blackened part of the prairie, looking for new feeding grounds and a place to live. At last they came to some tall grass where they could hide from their enemies. They found sunflower seeds to eat, but best of all they enjoyed the wild grapes hanging on a vine.

7

THE TEASING
MARSH HAWKS

The nights grew cooler as August faded into September. Prairie Chicken no longer tried to keep her five youngsters together. They mixed with others their own age and with the grown birds that often fed in nearby grain fields.

When the north wind brought the first crisp days of fall, the cocks again gathered on their historic courting grounds. Their booming calls were not as loud as in the spring, for it was not yet mating time.

One afternoon, while Prairie Chicken and the flock were sunning on a southern slope, two

marsh hawks appeared overhead. Instantly
Prairie Chicken crouched with the others in the
high grass.

The bluish-gray hawks circled around. They
halted in midair for a few seconds. Then they
swooped down and came within a hairsbreadth
of the prairie chickens, but did not strike at

them. With a few easy wing beats the large birds rose in the air to dive once more.

They did this several times and seemed to enjoy teasing the frightened prairie chickens until the noise from an approaching helicopter caught their attention. The large craft with its whirling blades was heading in the direction of the hawks.

Screaming, the birds gave up their teasing and flew away. They beat their wings rapidly to keep ahead of the big noisy machine.

Finally one hawk alighted on a fence post. A few moments later the second hawk landed on another post nearby. With feathers drawn closely about them they sat on their perches and looked around. As time went by, they did not go back to tease the prairie chickens. They preened their plumage instead.

Meanwhile Prairie Chicken kept a careful watch. She was ready to hide once more if the marsh hawks returned.

8

THE STORM

More weeks slipped by. Winter came with brisk winds to the coastal prairie of Texas.

Prairie Chicken had been roosting on the ground in the high grass at night. Now, as dusk was falling, she noticed white beads of sleet mixed with driving rain. Prairie Chicken had never seen sleet before since winters were generally mild on the prairie where she lived.

Faster and faster the icy drops came down. Prairie Chicken decided to roost with some hens on a knoll. She tucked her bill under her feathers and went to sleep.

The wind blew and howled. Low areas of the prairie were covered with rain and sleet. Then, just as suddenly as the storm came, it stopped.

In a little while a full moon shone in the heavens.

Prairie Chicken still slept on the knoll, looking like a ball of feathers. Except for the whistling of the sharp wind, all was still around her.

Suddenly a huge snorting cow awoke Prairie Chicken and the other hens with a start. She was looking for a dry bed and had found the knoll.

With a whirr of wings the flock flew in all directions. Prairie Chicken landed in a low place where the water was shallow. She waded through it, dragging her wings and struggled to the tops of taller clumps of grass. There she sat, still alive, but thoroughly chilled.

Early the next morning, when Prairie Chicken set out to feed, she found that some of her companions who had roosted with her on the knoll were not as fortunate as she. They had dropped into deep water, and they had drowned since chickens cannot swim.

Prairie Chicken walked slowly by the dead hens. Then she moved on to look for food on dry land.

9

MORE FLIGHTS

A feeling of spring was in the air now. The days grew longer, and a south wind swayed the fresh green grasses of the prairie. Male birds began courting females. A boat-tailed grackle showed off his plumage and made loud noises as he serenaded his ladylove. Two scissortail flycatchers chased each other, opening and closing their long forked tails and flashing the rosy lining of their handsome wings. A mourning dove spread his wings wide and sailed overhead in graceful turns. Meadowlarks were singing all around.

Prairie Chicken listened to the meadowlarks as she preened her dark and light brown barred feathers in the sunlight.

At dawn the next morning another sound attracted her attention—the booming calls of male prairie chickens.

Prairie Chicken with other hens visited the courting grounds but did not stay long.

A few days later Prairie Chicken wandered over to the courting grounds again. This time she chose a mate, a handsome cock who had showed off to win her favor.

In a little while Prairie Chicken set out to find a place for a new nest. She roamed through the high grass until she came near a fence. The earth was soft there, just right for her to scoop out a hollow.

As she started working, a grasshopper jumped in front of her. Prairie Chicken was so busy pecking at the soil that she did not see the tiny creature. Even a caterpillar crawling nearby failed to get her attention.

But after she had lined her nest and laid an egg in it, a loud noise made her jerk up her head in alarm. A tractor driven by a farmer was coming in her direction.

It moved over the land, pulling a mowing machine that was cutting down the high grass so greatly needed by prairie chickens.

Closer and closer came the tractor with its diesel engine.

Prairie Chicken's feathers stood on edge, but she did not budge. She wanted to stay near her nest.

Before long the noisy tractor was only a few yards away from her.

Prairie Chicken waited a little longer. Then, with a whirr of wings, she flew off, landing a short distance away. No high grass was there, only bare ground that another farmer had plowed for crops.

Prairie Chicken looked around. Catching sight of some other hens who had also been driven away from their nests by tractors, she joined them. They stood together and uttered soft noises as if they were talking over their troubles.

Soon the small flock decided to go elsewhere. They flew farther, passing more land that had been plowed.

Finally they saw tall grass. Prairie Chicken was the first to land in it. She was at home now. Quickly she scooped out a hollow in soft soil and lined it with dead weeds.

As twilight shadows deepened over the prairie,

Prairie Chicken roosted on the ground in the high grass.

The next day she listened for the sound of the dreaded tractor, but only the wind blowing the grasses broke the stillness. Satisfied, Prairie Chicken laid an egg in her new nest.

Three weeks later she laid the tenth egg. She fluffed out her feathers to keep the eggs warm. Although her plumage blended with the color of the land and grass around her, and thus helped to hide her, she kept a watchful eye for enemies.

In about three weeks ten chicks broke through the eggshells. Prairie Chicken gathered her babies under her wings. As soon as their down was dry, she would take her second family on their first outing.

BIBLIOGRAPHY

Allen, Arthur A. *Stalking Birds with Color Camera.* Washington, D. C.: National Geographic Society, 1951.

Allen, Durward L. *The Life of Prairies and Plains,* New York: McGraw-Hill, Inc., 1967.

Bent, Arthur Cleveland. *Life Histories of North American Gallinacious Birds,* New York: Dover Publications, Inc., 1963.

Butcher, Devereux. *Exploring our National Wildlife Refuges.* Boston: Houghton Mifflin, Co., 1963.

Cottam, Clarence. "Is the Attwater Prairie Chicken Doomed?" *Audubon Magazine,* November-December 1962. New York: National Audubon Society.

Gilliard, Thomas E. *Living Birds of the World*. Garden City, New York: Doubleday Co., 1958.

Hofsinde, Robert. *Indian Hunting*. New York: William Morrow & Co., 1962.

Laycock, George. *The Sign of the Flying Goose,* Garden City, New York: The Natural History Press, 1965.

Lehmann, V. W. *Attwater's Prairie. Its life history and management*. North America Fauna 57. Washington, D. C.: U.S. Government Printing Office, 1941.

National Audubon Society. *The Audubon Nature Encyclopedia*. Philadelphia-New York: Curtis Pub. Co., 1965.

Pearson, Gilbert T. *Birds of America*. Garden City, New York: Garden City Pub. Co., 1936.

Rand, Austin L. *American Water and Game Birds*. New York: E. P. Dutton & Co., 1956.

Schwartz, Charles. *Ecology of the Prairie Chicken in Missouri*. Columbia: University of Missouri, 1945.

Wetmore, Alexander. *Water, Prey and Game Birds of North America*. Washington, D. C.: National Geographic Society, 1965.

MARY ADRIAN

Miss Adrian graduated from Great Neck High School, Great Neck, Long Island, and studied at New York University. She was born in Sewickley, Pennsylvania. She is married to Henry Jorgensen and lives in Salem, Oregon.

Her literary record is an impressive one. She has had nature stories and articles published in *Boys' Life, Country Gentleman, Farm Journal, Jack and Jill. The Grade Teacher, Trails for Juniors* (Methodist Sunday School Paper) and *The Christian Science Monitor*. A nature column by her ran in the Sunday Magazine Section of the *Boston Post* for years, and she had a feature in *House Beautiful* called *Did You Know?* which dealt with unusual facts of nature.

Besides this she has published the following nature books: *Garden Spider, Honeybee, Fiddler Crab,* and *Gray Squirrel* (Holiday House), and many mystery stories based on nature information. See the complete list of her books opposite the title page.

The author and her husband are both members of the American Ornithologists Union, the National Audubon Society and the National Wildlife Federation.

GENEVIEVE VAUGHAN-JACKSON

Born in England, the artist spent the years from 1920 to 1926 in the west of Ireland in the depths of the country. This interlude was followed by school in England, after which there were two years of art school in Paris. She lived with a French family, and spent summers in the Alps with them, climbing and sketching.

In 1937, she came to the United States to teach art at the Foote School in New Haven where she enjoyed working with the children very much. During World War II she had a war job in the drafting room of a marine engineering company, and after that took up freelance art work, finally landing in the field of children's books.

Her husband is John Shimer, professor of geology at Brooklyn College. They live in New York City.

Miss Vaughan-Jackson has written and illustrated two books of her own: *Animals and Men in Armor* and *Mountains of Fire, an Introduction to the Science of Volcanos.*